DIGGING UP THE PAST

TERRA-COTTA ARMY

BY ABBY DOTY

WWW.APEXEDITIONS.COM

Copyright © 2026 by Apex Editions, Mendota Heights, MN 55120. All rights reserved. No part of this book may be reproduced or utilized in any form or by any means without written permission from the publisher.

Apex is distributed by North Star Editions:
sales@northstareditions.com | 888-417-0195

Produced for Apex by Red Line Editorial.

Photographs ©: Shutterstock Images, cover, 4–5, 13, 14–15, 20–21, 22–23, 29; iStockphoto, 1, 24, 27; Nian Zeng/Gamma-Rapho/Getty Images, 7; Daniele Darolle/Sygma/Getty Images, 8–9; Fine Art Images/Heritage Images/Hulton Archive/Getty Images, 10–11; Jonas Walzberg/picture-alliance/dpa/AP Images, 12; Zhang Yuan/Color China Photo/AP Images, 16–17; Daniele Darolle/Sygma/Getty Images, 18; Beibaoke/Alamy, 19; Linda Buckley/Flickr, 25

Library of Congress Control Number: 2025930917

ISBN
979-8-89250-536-9 (hardcover)
979-8-89250-572-7 (paperback)
979-8-89250-642-7 (ebook pdf)
979-8-89250-608-3 (hosted ebook)

Printed in the United States of America
Mankato, MN
082025

NOTE TO PARENTS AND EDUCATORS

Apex books are designed to build literacy skills in striving readers. Exciting, high-interest content attracts and holds readers' attention. The text is carefully leveled to allow students to achieve success quickly. Additional features, such as bolded glossary words for difficult terms, help build comprehension.

CHAPTER 1
HIDDEN SOLDIERS 4

CHAPTER 2
THE EMPEROR'S ARMY 10

CHAPTER 3
A GIANT FIND 16

CHAPTER 4
STUDYING THE STATUES 22

COMPREHENSION QUESTIONS • 28
GLOSSARY • 30
TO LEARN MORE • 31
ABOUT THE AUTHOR • 31
INDEX • 32

CHAPTER 1

HIDDEN SOLDIERS

In March 1974, farmers in China dig a well. They find arrowheads under the dirt. They find pieces of pottery, too.

Farmers found ancient items near Xi'an, China. People have lived in this area for thousands of years.

The farmers tell some **archaeologists**. The scientists collect the pottery pieces. They put the pieces back together. The pieces make two life-size statues of soldiers.

FAST FACT
Some of the pottery pieces were the size of fingernails.

Zhao Kangmin was one of the archaeologists who studied the clay soldiers.

The scientists know that China's first emperor is buried nearby. So, workers begin digging. After a few months, they discover a huge **tomb**. They find hundreds of **terra-cotta** soldiers inside.

A BIG JOB

Most of the clay soldiers stand about 6 feet (1.8 m) tall. Some weigh more than 600 pounds (270 kg). Scientists think about 700,000 workers made them. The work took more than 30 years.

Between 1978 and 1984, scientists found more than 1,500 pieces of terra-cotta soldiers.

CHAPTER 2

THE EMPEROR'S ARMY

The terra-cotta army is a big group of statues. Qin Shi Huang had them built. He ruled as China's emperor from 221 to 210 BCE.

Qin Shi Huang was the first emperor of China.

Some pits near Qin Shi Huang's tomb held weapons such as spears and arrows.

Qin Shi Huang believed in an **afterlife**. So, he built himself a large tomb. Many pits surrounded it. He filled them with things he might want in the afterlife.

IN THE TOMB

Some pits held statues of musicians and birds. Scientists think these were for **entertainment** in the afterlife. Some pits held **armor**. Others held horses or **chariots**.

Some of the horses and chariots in the pits were made from bronze.

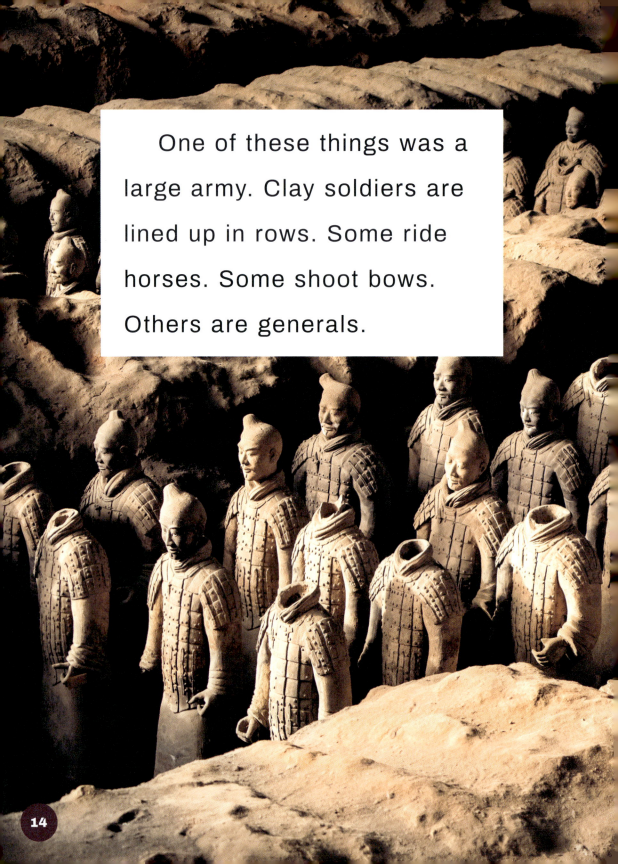

One of these things was a large army. Clay soldiers are lined up in rows. Some ride horses. Some shoot bows. Others are generals.

FAST FACT
Each soldier is unique. They all have different clothes and faces.

▲ Most of the terra-cotta soldiers face east. It's like they're guarding the emperor from enemies.

15

CHAPTER 3

A GIANT FIND

Scientists have been digging near Qin Shi Huang's tomb for decades. They have found more than 600 pits. The site covers 22 square miles (57 sq km).

The terra-cotta soldiers can break easily. So, scientists must dig carefully.

Scientists think the pits may hold as many as 8,000 terra-cotta soldiers.

People have uncovered more than 2,000 terra-cotta soldiers so far. Most are broken. Finding and fitting together the pieces can take years.

FIRE

Scientists found ashes and burn marks in some of the pits. Old **records** show that people fought against the Qin rulers. Some scientists think these people started the fires.

Qin Er Shi was the second and last Qin ruler. His tomb is in Xi'an, China.

Many pits and statues remain buried. To find them, scientists use **radar**. They scan the ground. Radar shows them where to dig and what they might find.

FAST FACT

The dig site has a museum. Visitors can see the pits and soldiers.

Millions of people visit the terra-cotta army each year.

CHAPTER 4

STUDYING THE STATUES

Researchers studied the statues. They learned how people made them. Some body parts, such as the hands, are all the same. Workers likely used molds for these parts.

The statues have eight different head shapes. A mold made each one.

Workers added details to the faces and clothes. They used large kilns to harden the clay. Then they painted and buried the statues.

Kilns are used in many types of pottery. They use fire to heat clay and harden it.

Bits of paint remain on some statues. Scientists can see what colors people used.

DIGGING DEEP

Most statues were buried 15 to 20 feet (4.6 to 6.1 m) underground. The pits had wood ceilings. Logs helped hold up the walls.

The statues stand how soldiers would have stood in battle. So, they help people learn how the Qin army fought. For instance, soldiers with extra armor guarded the sides and backs of groups.

FAST FACT

Hairstyles showed the soldiers' roles. For example, soldiers with ponytails carried crossbows.

Depending on what weapons they used, soldiers had buns, braids, or ponytails.

COMPREHENSION QUESTIONS

Write your answers on a separate piece of paper.

1. Write a few sentences explaining the main ideas of Chapter 2.

2. Do you believe in an afterlife? Why or why not?

3. Which parts of the statues were likely made with molds?
   - A. their faces
   - B. their hands
   - C. their hair

4. What might happen if scientists didn't use radar?
   - A. They could spend more time digging up empty areas.
   - B. They could spend less time looking for underground items.
   - C. They could dig up underground items more quickly.

5. What does **unique** mean in this book?

*Each soldier is **unique**. They all have different clothes and faces.*

    A. very small
    B. exactly the same
    C. unlike any other

6. What does **researchers** mean in this book?

***Researchers** studied the statues. They learned how people made them.*

    A. people who study things
    B. people who build things
    C. people who break things

Answer key on page 32.

GLOSSARY

afterlife
A place some people believe spirits go after death.

archaeologists
People who study long-ago times, often by digging up things from the past.

armor
Coverings that keep people or things safe.

chariots
Two-wheeled carts pulled by horses or other animals.

entertainment
Things that people do for fun or enjoyment.

radar
A system that sends out radio waves to locate objects.

records
Writings that tell about something that happened in the past.

terra-cotta
Made from reddish-brown clay fired in a kiln.

tomb
A space where a dead person is buried.

BOOKS

Cooke, Tim. *Pompeii and Other Legendary Ancient Places*. Lerner Publications, 2024.

Murray, Julie. *Terracotta Army*. Abdo Publishing, 2022.

Van, R. L. *China*. Abdo Publishing, 2023.

ONLINE RESOURCES

Visit **www.apexeditions.com** to find links and resources related to this title.

ABOUT THE AUTHOR

Abby Doty is a writer, editor, and booklover from Minnesota.

INDEX

A
afterlife, 12–13
archaeologists, 6
armor, 13, 26

C
China, 4, 8, 10

E
emperor, 8, 10

F
farmers, 4, 6
fires, 19

M
museum, 20

P
pits, 12–13, 16, 19–20, 25

Q
Qin Shi Huang, 10, 12, 16

S
scientists, 6, 8, 13, 19–20
soldiers, 6, 8, 14–15, 18, 20, 26
statues, 6, 10, 13, 20, 22, 24–26

T
tomb, 8, 12–13, 16

W
workers, 8, 22, 24

ANSWER KEY:
1. Answers will vary; 2. Answers will vary; 3. B; 4. A; 5. C; 6. A